Expert Pet Care

CARING for Hamsters

A 4D BOOK

by Tammy Gagne

Consultant:
Jennifer Zablotny, DVM
Member, American Veterinary Medical Association

PEBBLE
a capstone imprint

Download the Capstone **4D** app!

- Ask an adult to download the Capstone 4D app.
- Scan the cover and stars inside the book for additional content.

When you scan a spread, you'll find fun extra stuff to go with this book! You can also find these things on the web at www.capstone4D.com using the password: hamstercare.27407

First Facts are published by Pebble
1710 Roe Crest Drive, North Mankato, Minnesota 56003
www.mycapstone.com

Library of Congress Cataloging-in-Publication Data
is available on the Library of Congress website.

ISBN 978-1-5435-2740-7 (library binding)
ISBN 978-1-5435-2746-9 (paperback)
ISBN 978-1-5435-2752-0 (ebook pdf)

Editorial Credits
Marissa Kirkman, editor; Sarah Bennett, designer; Tracy Cummins, media researcher; Laura Manthe, production specialist

Photo Credits
Alamy: Top-Pet-Pics, 17; Capstone Studio: Karon Dubke, 4, 5, 13; iStockphoto: Antagain, 14 Right; Shutterstock: AlexBukharov, 23, Allocricetulus, 21 Top, AtiwatPhotography, 19, ekmelica, Design Element, Elya Vatel, 3, fantom_rd, 20, Igor Kovalchuk, 14 Left, Jackal photography, 12, Jane September, 8, Kurashova, 21 Bottom, Lepas, 10, Natalia7, Back Cover, 24, Punyaphat Larpsomboon, 18, santypan, 15, Steve Design, 16, Viachaslau Kraskouski, Cover, Vicky du Toit, 7, Victor FlowerFly, 9, Vishnevskiy Vasily, 21 Middle, Weerawat Promchai, 11; SuperStock: Adrianko/Cultura Limited, 6.

Printed in the United States of America.
PA017

Table of Contents

Your New Pet Hamster

Do you enjoy watching hamsters run around their cages? Hamsters make great first pets. You can buy these tiny animals at most pet stores.

Owning a hamster is a big **responsibility**. Before buying one, you should learn all about this **rodent**. Knowing how to care for a hamster will help you keep your pet happy and healthy.

There are different sizes and kinds of hamsters. You will need to choose a hamster that is right for you and your family.

responsibility—a duty or a job

rodent—a mammal with long front teeth used for gnawing; rats, mice, and squirrels are rodents

Supplies You Will Need

Your hamster will need a cage. A hamster's sharp teeth can **gnaw** through plastic cages. A covered glass **aquarium** works best. A wire cage can also be used for larger hamsters.

Place **bedding** inside the cage. Aspen wood **shavings** work great. Your hamster needs a food dish, water bottle, toys, and an exercise wheel. You can also add plastic tubes for your hamster to run through.

gnaw—to wear away by repeated biting or nibbling with the teeth

aquarium—a glass tank where pets, including hamsters, hermit crabs, and fish, are kept

bedding—materials used to make an animal's bed; hamsters use aspen wood shavings and shredded paper for bedding

shaving—a thin slice or piece; wood shavings are used as bedding for some animals

FACT
Hamsters clean themselves in dust. You can find this at your pet supply store.

Bringing Your Hamster Home

Give your hamster time to explore its new cage. Picking your hamster up too soon may scare it or cause it to bite. Start by placing your hand in the cage. Let the animal come to you and sniff your hand. Soon you will be able to pick it up safely. Be careful if you have larger pets. Dogs and cats can hurt hamsters.

FACT
Holding a treat can
help get your hamster
to come to you.

What Do Hamsters Eat?

Feed your hamster **pellets** from the pet supply store. This food is made with the **vitamins** hamsters need. Most hamsters eat at night. Keep fresh food and water in the cage at all times.

Hamsters also eat fruits and vegetables. But hamsters do not eat much. A tiny piece of apple or carrot is plenty. Remove any food your pet doesn't eat the same day.

Never give your hamster onions, potatoes, or oranges. These foods can make a hamster sick.

pellet—a small, hard piece of food; pellets give animals the nutrition they need

vitamin—a nutrient that helps keep people and animals healthy

Cleaning Your Hamster's Cage

Clean your hamster's cage and tubes once a week. Start by removing the shavings. After cleaning, add fresh shavings. Wash and refill your pet's food dish and water bottle.

Have a family member hold your pet while you clean. You may also put your pet in an exercise ball. Hamsters get exercise running around inside one of these round toys.

An easy way to get your hamster in its ball is by placing the open ball inside the cage. As soon as your pet climbs inside, you can then fasten the lid.

Keeping Your Hamster Healthy

Healthy hamsters have bright eyes and soft fur. A hamster that doesn't eat enough or sleeps too much may be sick.

If your hamster gets sick, take it to a **veterinarian**. You must be sure the vet treats small animals, including hamsters. Some vets only treat larger animals.

A hamster's hair may be long or short. Hamsters also come in many colors such as black, brown, or white.

 veterinarian—a doctor trained to take care of animals

Life with a Hamster

Some small animals enjoy living in groups. But hamsters prefer to live alone. Keeping two or more hamsters in the same cage can lead to fights.

A hamster's front teeth never stop growing. Hamsters chew often to keep their teeth short. Give your pet plenty of toys to chew on.

FACT
Hamster chew toys look different than other pet toys. Many are made from colorful wooden blocks or sticks.

Your Hamster Through the Years

Hamsters usually live about two to three years. Make sure your hamster has healthy food, lots of exercise, and a clean cage. This will give your pet the best chance at a long life.

Hamsters are mostly active at night. However, they become less active as they get older. They may sleep more and play a bit less.

Hamster Body Language

A hamster's **behavior** says a lot about how it is feeling. When a hamster is tired, it folds its ear against its head. Picking it up at this time could cause it to bite. Hamsters stretch and squeak when they are happy. They may be more open to being held at this time. Always be careful and move slowly when holding your pet.

behavior—the way a person or an animal acts

Types of Hamsters

The most common types of pet hamsters:

- Campbell dwarf hamsters
- Chinese hamsters
- Robo hamsters
- Russian dwarf hamsters
- Syrian hamsters (also called teddy bear hamsters)
- Winter white hamsters

Glossary

aquarium (uh-KWAYR-ee-uhm)—a glass tank where pets, including hamsters, hermit crabs, and fish, are kept

bedding (BED-ing)—materials used to make an animal's bed; hamsters use aspen wood shavings and shredded paper for bedding

behavior (bee-HAY-vyuhr)—the way a person or an animal acts

gnaw (NAW)—to wear away by repeated biting or nibbling with the teeth

pellet (PEL-it)—a small, hard piece of food; pellets give animals the nutrition they need

responsibility (ri-spon-suh-BIL-uh-tee)—a duty or a job

rodent (ROHD-uhnt)—a mammal with long front teeth used for gnawing; rats, mice, and squirrels are rodents

shaving (SHEY-ving)—a thin slice or piece; wood shavings are used as bedding for some animals

veterinarian (vet-ur-uh-NER-ee-uhn)—a doctor trained to take care of animals

vitamin (VYE-tuh-min)—a nutrient that helps keep people and animals healthy

Read More

Bartlett, Patricia. *The Hamster Handbook*. Barron's Pet Handbooks, Second Edition. Hauppauge, N.Y.: Barron's Educational Series, Inc., 2015.

Gardeski, Christina Mia. *Hamsters: Questions and Answers*. Pet Questions and Answers. North Mankato, Minn.: Capstone Press, 2017.

Meister, Cari. *Hamsters*. My First Pet. Minneapolis: Bullfrog Books, 2015.

Internet Sites

Use FactHound to find
Internet sites related to this book.

Visit *www.facthound.com*

Just type in 9781543527407 and go.

Critical Thinking Questions

1. Why would a plastic cage not be a good home for a hamster?

2. What are some daily jobs you will need to do to care for your pet hamster?

3. How can your hamster get the exercise it needs to stay healthy?

Index